Leadership 101: Don't be a Dick

9 Steps To Building and Leading a Self-Managing Team

ANDY NISEVIC

Leadership 101: Don't be a Dick
9 Steps to Building and Leading a Self-Managing Team

ISBN: 978-1-7390907-0-8 Paperback

Published by: Inspired By Publishing

Cover Design By: Tanya Grant – The TNG Designs Group Limited

Contents

Introduction

Who gets to decide if you're a "dick"?

Is it something we get to decide for ourselves? Or is it something other people decide?

Ultimately, it's down to other people.

We can't be naive, there are narcissistic people out there who blindly believe that everything they say and do is golden – irrespective of any and all feedback given to them.

In my experience though, a good 80% of managers with reputations of being a "dick", are just ordinary people, doing the best they can with the skills, knowledge, and resources they have at their disposal.

Most are good people; outside of work they're loved by their friends and family.

Inside of work, they were promoted for being good at their job, but haven't been provided the proper training and support required to be good leaders.

The title of this book: "Don't be a Dick" was designed to grab your attention. Not, as some have joked to be confrontational, or to generate sales.

The very simple reason is, in my humble opinion, it's the foundation that underpins great leadership.

In every conversation we have, every decision we make, if our intention is to do the absolute best we can, for our staff **AND** our organisation, with the skills, knowledge, and resources available to us at the time, it'll be very difficult to be accused of being a "dick". Or, if you prefer a more professional language, not be a manager who breeds toxicity.

I can remember 13th June 2016. A small Royal Air Force Station just outside Lincoln. I was a newly promoted Flight Sergeant in the RAF, which is the equivalent to a department head in civilian terms.

This was my first day at my new unit, in my new rank. My boss told me in our first 1:1 that he needed me to "get a grip" of the people because discipline, morale, and productivity were at an all-time low.

This wasn't news to me. I knew quite a few of the people who'd be working with me; I'd been in communication with them before arriving. I'd already started to get an appreciation of what was going on.

The unit I'd been posted to was responsible for supporting the air defence of the UK, as well as providing combat training for overseas operations.

It's essential work, and very repetitive, which quickly becomes extremely monotonous.

Maintaining motivation of even the most enthusiastic of staff, by even the most skilled of leaders, is a challenge.

The trap many of the leaders had fallen into was focusing all their efforts trying to improve morale down the chain, rather than keeping the bigger picture in mind.

This is an incredibly easy trap to fall into, because morale is such an important factor for any workplace, be it military or civilian.

The trouble with it being the only focus, is it tends to result in trying to people please. All efforts are put into trying to give people what they want, and forgetting about what's needed.

Want vs need often conflict with each other. It resulted in a huge divide between the people responsible for leading the people, and the unit executive staff.

Communication up and down the chain wasn't just poor, it was non-existent. Their intent was positive for the staff, so they were liked by the people, but because focus on what the unit needed wasn't there, effectiveness was very low.

My challenge, despite morale being low, was to start improving productivity. You see, people pleasing is an impossible task.

Pleasing one person often means having to disappoint someone else. I.e., multiple people wanting to take overlapping leave, when you need a minimum number of people each day.

Morale isn't built by giving someone what they want. It's built by giving people the opportunity to accomplish something.

Providing them with meaningful work and giving them the chance to develop and flourish professionally.

The thing that goes hand in hand with low morale is lethargy. In simple terms, lethargy is an unwillingness to do anything productive, despite being incredibly bored and frustrated. The desire to accomplish something is there, but the drive to do something isn't.

The approach I took was a huge risk. I told people what I actually thought. I was bluntly honest. It upset some people and they saw me as a dick. To others, it was a breath of fresh air.

Those people who appreciated my blunt honesty started to thrive. Then, others started to recognise an opportunity to improve their lot. They started to respond positively. Over the course of around six months, things really improved.

While my intent was to do the absolute best I could for the people, I knew my approach wouldn't make me popular. There were many people, in the beginning, who didn't like my approach. However, because the intent was positive, and it combined the needs of the people **AND** the unit, the result was a positive one.

When I moved onto a different squadron, I would regularly have people asking to join me there - including those who initially saw me as a bit of a dick.

You see, you can't control what other people will think of you. Ironically, when you focus too hard on trying to be liked, effectiveness plummets. So can people's respect for you.

When you focus on giving people what they, and the organisation needs to flourish, success follows. The hard thing is challenging your own bias, assumptions, and beliefs to learn what the real need is.

I've deliberately written this book using one of my favourite acronyms – KISS - Keep It Simple Stupid.

Not because people are stupid but to simplify the academic models and theories. Leaders can quickly and easily apply these proven techniques to their leadership style and stand the best chance of not only being an incredibly effective leader, but one who's liked and respected, i.e., not a dick.

Happy reading.

Andy Nisevic
Author
Founder & Director of One Degree Training & Coaching Ltd.
www.onedegree.uk
info@onedegree.uk

To lead others is to push the boundaries of what they believe is possible.

Chapter 1

The Power of Effective Communication

Yes, get those bingo cards at the ready, here's the first buzzword - communication! Even better, a "buzz-phrase" - effective communication!

But there is a reason why I've chosen to open with this as the first chapter.

It doesn't matter what level you're at in the workplace, whether you're a man or woman, executive of a multinational corporation, MD of a small business, or a brand-new emerging leader and everything in between.

When you boil all our leadership challenges down to a single root cause, communication lies at the centre of it.

Section 1: The Importance of Non-Verbal Communication

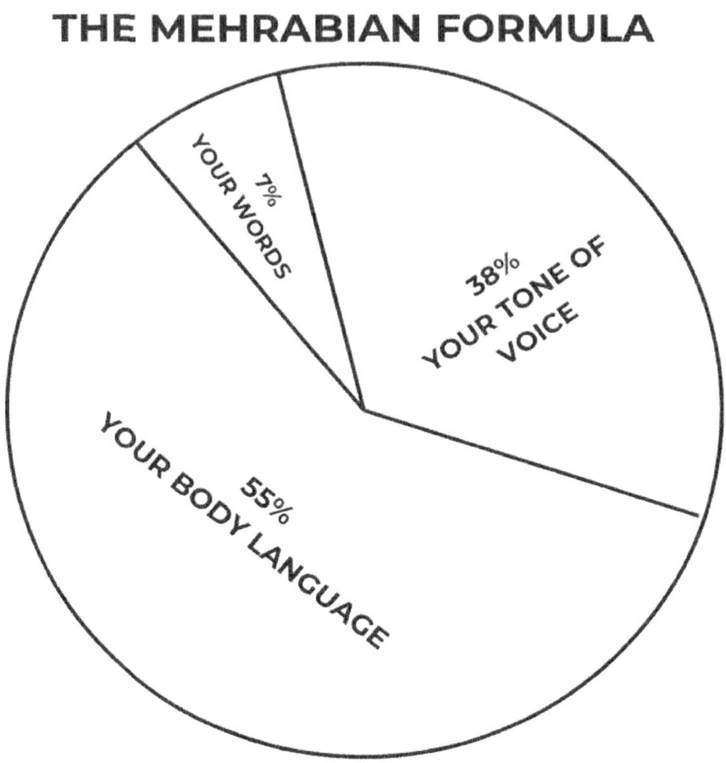

Mehrabian Theory is an extremely common theory of communication. Its author, Alfred Mehrabian, published his work in 1967; it's believed to tell us that 55% of our communication comes from body language, 38% from tonality, and only 7% from the actual words we use.

The truth is, Mehrabian wasn't really saying that. He even admits that the experiment that publication was based on, was far too narrow.

The myth behind Mehrabian is that non-verbal communication is far more important than the words themselves.

This is too simplistic; but, let me ask you this …

Have you ever misinterpreted an email or text message? Or, have any of yours, however innocent, caused a ruckus?

Mehrabian's Theory is a really useful tool to understand why that's happening - at a basic level anyway.

There are multiple factors involved in communication. Our mood, our feelings toward the person we're communicating with, our current stress levels, to name but a few.

Of course, all of this is going on with the other person too. All of these will affect our volume, tone, pitch, dictation, body language, and micro-indicators within our facial expressions.

Our subconscious mind is reading all of these simultaneously, all while our conscious mind is busy hearing the words being said.

Section 2: The Impact of Tone & Body Language

When we communicate via words only, it's almost impossible to read them with any other perspective than our own emotional state.

If we're stressed, anxious, or have negative feelings towards the individual, it's all too easy to read the words in a negative way. Of course, the opposite is also true.

If we're in a positive frame of mind, it's all too easy to miss the urgency of a situation.

This is where the non-verbal cues become so vital. Often, words only say so much, it's the passion and emotion that they're said with that relay the real intent behind them.

A simple joke told over text message can result in a relationship ending (speaking from experience there!), but one that's even more risqué said in person, with the humorous tone, the twinkle in the eye, the mischievousness written all over the face, can relieve tension and improve the relationship, even if only temporarily.

The same is true in the workplace too. A bland, factual email, sent by a manager who's seen to be putting pressure on their staff, could be interpreted as stressful.

But that manager could just quite as easily be sending around a simple update to inform their staff of the current situation.

The absence of the non-verbal cues makes it incredibly easy to misunderstand each other.

See the end of the chapter for an exercise that demonstrates this.

Section 3: Exploring Various Forms of Communication

There are many different ways in which we communicate. They all have both advantages and disadvantages:

- Verbal communication
- Written communication
- Visual communication
- Non-verbal communication
- Mass communication
- Group communication
- Feedback communication

The modern workplace looks nothing like it used to. It no longer requires expensive and time consuming (not even considering the environmental impact) travel to see international partners or customers.

Many people have options to work from home, or take jobs in cities hundreds of miles away and work in a shared workspace.

Modern technology means that people with mental health and learning difficulties, or one of the myriads of personality disorders, but with certain talents, can gain meaningful employment where once they would have been either shunned, or wouldn't have sought it out.

There are many other benefits too, lifestyle, mental health, childcare, individual strengths, can all be accommodated through the technology that's becoming more and more standard.

With all of this in mind though, we have to consider section 1 to this chapter - the importance of non-verbal communication, and section 2 - the impact of tone and body language.

Most of the electronic forms of communications we use are excellent at conveying the words.

We can edit information to make sure it says exactly what we want it to say, and send it out to huge numbers of people simultaneously at just a click of the button.

The important thing there though is that we make it say exactly what **WE** want it to say, unfortunately we can't control how the recipient(s) will interpret it, as discussed earlier in the chapter.

That seems to suggest that face-to-face communication is the only way to go, doesn't it?!

However, a study commissioned by Microsoft in 2015, concluded that, on average, when being spoken to, a human being only maintains focus for approximately 8 seconds before the brain goes on a tangent of its own.

That's not because human beings are dumb, or lack focus, it's because our brains are doing what they're designed to do. They're going back through our memories to find an example that adds context to what's being said.

Paradoxically, it's doing that to help us understand, but it results in us often missing vital information, or coming across as though we're not listening.

The answer therefore is a blended approach.

Have you ever passed information to someone who, once you've finished speaking, has asked you to put it all in an email? Frustrating right?!

Whether they knew why what they were doing was right doesn't matter.

The truth is, it's the best way to gain the fullest understanding possible.

The passion, emotion, urgency, etc, has been passed through face-to-face interaction; the words that help the individual(s) remember the key points are in the email.

This is one of the key reasons why remote or hybrid working solutions create such a debate, and so many more leadership challenges.

Irrespective of the technology available, video calls aren't the same as face-to-face communication for building trust, respect, understanding, and empowerment.

While there are some that thrive like that, there are many others who don't - but that could be a book in itself!

The important thing for managers, at all levels, is to understand how human beings communicate, and how to ensure that we communicate in a way the other person needs us to, not how we need them to.

Post-chapter activity:

Try this experiment with your team. Repeat a phrase 3 times, using the exact words, but with a completely different tone.

For example:

Imagine a team member has come to you confessing they've messed up and it's going to cost the company approximately £5,000 to rectify.

Speak the phrase: "you bloody idiot", 3 times using a different tone each time. I.e.:

1. Nonchalant
2. Humorous

3. Angry

After each instance, ask your team to write down their interpretation of your feelings on the matter.

What did each team member write down? You'll find that some will interpret it the way you intended. Others will read it in a different way.

That's because our interpretation of other people's communication is as much down to what we're thinking and feeling as them.

Leaders need followers. Followership is a choice, give them something worth following.

Chapter 2

Active Listening: The Art of Understanding

That's got to be 2/2 in the buzzword/buzz-phrase bingo, right?!

An extremely common misconception when it comes to being an effective communicator, is the assumption that it's about how we pass information to others.

Around 80% of good communication is the art of listening. It's amazing how much we'll learn if we just zip our lips and let other people talk.

That's why this is step 2 on our journey towards great leadership.

You can always tell when someone has been on an active listening course because, all of a sudden, they start using what are known as 'conversational lubricators'. Sounds like ohhhh, ahhh, and uh-huh, with lots of head nodding, and "go on", or "I see" being repeated.

I know that was me in my early days of developing. The trouble is, I often became conscious of the noises I was making, which led to me feeling self-conscious.

I started to think to myself, have I made that noise too much, which one should I make next.

Ironically, the efforts I was making to be an active listener, meant I wasn't actually listening because I was in my own head.

That said, when you get it right, it's immensely powerful.

Section 1: The Essence of Active Listening

Active listening is a term that gets used frequently. True active listening is something that can be very hard to perfect, it's tiring, and takes patience and practice.

Listening is actually interactive. It requires good judgement to know when to interrupt to ask questions, and when to stay silent to give the other person the space to think.

The power of silence in conversation cannot be understated. It's extremely uncomfortable, and we have to fight our own urge to fill the silence.

However, when used correctly can be incredibly useful in gaining all the necessary information required from the conversation.

Section 2: The Levels of Listening

There are many, many, studies that suggest between 3 and 5 levels of listening.

The 3 level models, usually include all aspects of the 5 level ones, just merged into the others. The 5-level model breaks them all down:

THE 5 LEVELS OF LISTENING

1. Level 1 is when we simply aren't listening. We may be pretending to, but actually we're either still working away on our computer or thinking of something completely unrelated.

2. Level 2 listening is when we focus on a specific piece of information, then stop listening, because we've assumed we know what they're going to say.

3. At level 3 we have a related experience, or a desire to add our own perspective. We're hearing what's being and we're paying attention, but our primary intent is to wait for our turn to speak.

4. Level 4 listening requires a higher-level of attention, so we can apply the information to our decision making.

5. It's only at level 5 where we can be truly empathetic to what's being spoken. It requires our devoted attention. We need to ask questions to ensure we understand properly, we need to paraphrase to give the speaker assurance that we've understood, and it requires silence for them to get their information across.

At levels 1 to 3, the listener is only interested in their own agenda. Level 4 listening is good, because we're attempting to understand the information being passed.

Often though, full understanding can only be achieved when we recognise the emotion and urgency within the other person. Complete understanding, and maximum rapport, can only be achieved with level 5 listening.

The key to being a good active listener, and preventing the other person from leaving the conversation feeling as though you're a bit of a dick - just be quiet!

Ask questions to clarify information, paraphrase to ensure you've understood, and if you feel as though they've got more to say, chances are that you're right.

Them being quiet isn't an invitation for you to start speaking, it's just them figuring out what to say and how to say it.

Staying silent can be incredibly uncomfortable, but it's one of the most powerful weapons in your arsenal.

Here's a personal story about the power of silence.

It was Spring 2012, I was a Sergeant based at a small RAF Station just outside Lincoln (the same one as in the introduction). I headed up a team of around 20 or so people, on an operational squadron.

To protect confidence, I'm going to keep the information vague because there's a chance some of the readers of this book could be familiar with the circumstances.

Someone had been posted on to my team, coming in with a really good reputation. However, their performance conflicted with that reputation.

They were severely under-performing, to such a degree they were on the cusp of being determined as unsuitable for the post.

I didn't know this individual before they arrived on my team; such was their under-performance I deemed it necessary to hold a difficult conversation quite early.

The beginning of the conversation was very frustrating. They were polite and respectful, but obviously very uncomfortable.

This meant all I received in response to my questions was answers.

Their body language told me there was more than they were saying so asked a question along the lines of "what is it that you're not saying?".

This was a risk. They didn't know me, I didn't really know them. There hadn't been a lot of time to build trust beyond the basic level of "assumed" trust you'd have for a new line manager

It resulted in around 6-minutes of silence. This was incredibly uncomfortable. I was sweating profusely, the back of my shirt was soaking wet with it! I was so uncomfortable it physically hurt!

It was around 6-minutes, but felt like 6-hours! I rode it out though, and thank goodness I did!

I found out later that they had no idea the silence had lasted so long. From their perspective, it felt like less than a minute.

You see, they weren't deliberately being difficult or non-responsive. The silence was them figuring out what to say and how to say it, whilst also trying to work out if I was someone they could trust to say it to.

Thankfully they took a leap of faith in me. Everything they'd been managing came pouring out.

When I say "everything", what I mean is just so much awful "stuff" that you wouldn't wish even one of the things on anyone, let alone all of it at the same time.

Had I succumbed to my discomfort, which was incredibly tempting, they wouldn't have taken a chance on me. But because I gave them the space they needed, they decided to trust me.

I was able to sign post and support as needed; that individual went from someone on the verge of being removed from post (potentially a career killing move), to having a very successful career.

All because I stayed silent giving the time they needed to decide to share.

Post-chapter activity:

Next time you're in a 1:1 conversation with someone, try removing all thoughts, distractions and assumptions from your mind. It's not easy, here are some things you can do:

1. Intermittently paraphrase what they've just said. This shows that you're listening and you understand. It also allows them to recognise if you've misunderstood and clarify the information.

2. Ask clarification questions. Even if you don't feel as though you've misunderstood, it helps you be active in the conversation, without them seeing you as speaking over them. It mitigates the risk of you being distracted with your own thoughts and assumptions.

Chapter 3

The Psychology of Persuasion: Influencing Others Positively

Once you're able to communicate effectively, including being able to listen at least at a level 4, the next step is to recognise how to influence your staff to be motivated irrespective of the situation, or job you need them to do.

Every single one of us are motivated in different ways. Sometimes the difference is very subtle, sometimes it's huge.

The trick as a leader is to recognise what the individual requires, not how you prefer it.

There is an abundance of psychometric assessments on the market that will help you learn what your team member's preferences are.

Often, the benefits of them are very similar, they just use different language to suit different people.

If none of these psychometric assessments are available, there are various persuasive skills we can use to help us motivate our staff.

Something I like to say is "Leadership is a paradox; it's simultaneously the easiest and hardest thing in the world. It's easy because all you have to do is find out what motivates the people you're responsible for, and use that to help them achieve greatness.

It's the hardest because everyone is motivated in different ways". Even for the same person, what worked for them once, won't necessarily work another time.

One of the easiest ways to be seen as a dick in leadership, is to fail to find a way to truly motivate someone.

There are many debates over whether or not someone needs to be motivated or disciplined. For me, it's a chicken and egg situation. Someone could be hugely motivated to lose weight, for example, and regularly attend the gym.

However, if they lack the discipline to not only incorporate the good habits, but to also remove the bad ones, such as takeaways and sugary snacks, their success will be limited.

Conversely someone could be extremely disciplined in adhering to a strict diet, if they lack motivation to exercise and learn new healthy eating habits, the good work they did through dieting can be undone very soon after the regime ends.

Whichever way you look at it, both discipline and motivation are required for success in all walks of life. It really doesn't matter which one comes first, as long as one feeds the other.

In the workplace, a leader needs to find a way to both motivate their team(s) and instil within them the discipline to keep it up when times are tough.

There are 2-ways to do this: the carrot, and the stick.

Both of them can be extremely effective, in the right environment, with the right people. The main difference between the two is the people who prefer the stick, also respond well to the carrot. Those who prefer the carrot, rarely respond well to the stick.

That has nothing to do with being a good/bad, or a strong/weak person. It's purely down to their individual motivational values, their strengths, and what puts them into conflict.

For context, some of the biggest cry-babies I've ever come across, are those who use the stick to motivate people. They're always complaining that the "younger generations" don't have the resilience that they had. But, when the stick is used on them, they cry louder and longer than anyone.

The difference?

People with more resilience openly admit they don't appreciate the stick method. They'll also make it clear to the people trying to use it.

Those "old school", who are apparently a lot stronger, will whinge, and bitch, and moan, to whoever will listen – except the people who used it on them.

There is a huge difference between "putting up" with the stick, and being motivated by it. Some of the strongest, most resilient people I've come across have been of the younger generation.

Being willing to say "I don't accept this" is a hard thing to do, and takes a lot of courage.

Section 1: Understanding Persuasion Techniques

In 1984, a psychologist working out of Arizona State University, named Robert Cialdini, published a book called "The Psychology of Persuasion".

It explores the ways in which human beings can be persuaded to behave in one way or another. In the book, he introduced 6 key tactics people can use to influence decision making.

RECIPROCITY

The first of the principles is that of **reciprocity**. Put simply, the idea is that if you do something for someone, they're likely to want to do something for you.

In times gone by, it used to be very common that when someone moved into a new house, one of their neighbours would bring them a cooked meal.

The idea was the family would be so busy moving they wouldn't have had the chance to cook a family meal. Easier access to fast food and takeaways saw that die out, but numerous studies were conducted into this behaviour.

What the studies show was the act of doing something for someone else, not only generated positive feelings within the person receiving the gift, but also within the giver.

This feeling of positivity was associated with the individuals involved and it helped bring the communities together.

People liked each other more, just because someone brought a cooked meal. From the perspective of reciprocity, the studies also concluded that when we receive a gift, a favour, or a service, we develop a subconscious feeling of obligation.

This makes us want to be liked by the person doing the favour and we'll find any opportunity to return it.

From a leadership perspective, this means that if your intent as a leader is to always make people and their lived experience better, they will not only want to work hard for you, but they need to.

SCARCITY

Scarcity is a common technique used by salespeople and retailers to persuade you to make a buying decision quickly – just how long has the DFS sale been 'ending soon' for now? Another tactic is "last few remaining".

Whilst the principle of scarcity doesn't translate neatly into a method of influence that leaders can use, the idea behind scarcity is to generate a sense of urgency.

Urgency is certainly tactic leaders can use to good effect. When your workforce understands the importance of a certain task or project, how it will benefit them, and the organisational goals, you can generate a sense of urgency to ensure tight deadlines are met.

AUTHORITY

Authority in this writer's humble opinion is one of the two most dangerous forms of influence.

In 1961 a psychologist at Yale university called Stanley Milgram conducted an experiment into people's obedience to authority. It was called the Milgram Experiment and has become quite famous because of the ethical boundaries it crossed.

Participants of the experiment were split into two groups, those asking questions and those answering.

The group answering the questions has electrodes placed on their bodies and would receive an electric shock if they answered incorrectly.

The group asking the questions were responsible for initiating the shock by pressing a button. The two groups couldn't see each other but communicated over the radio.

The shocks started off as very mild but gradually increased to fatal levels. The scientists were present throughout the experiment, their white lab coats marking them as people with authority.

The scientist kept on telling the people asking the questions that they were doing no harm and should continue to increase the shock level. Which the experiment participants did.

It didn't matter how much the participants answering the questions screamed in pain, and begged for them to stop, because the people with authority said it was ok, they kept increasing the shocks.

Many of them delivered well over the level of electric shock that is fatal to human beings.

It was only after the experiment was over that the group asking the questions were told that the other group were paid actors and they hadn't actually been electrocuting them.

The point was made though, human beings are capable of deliberately inflicting extreme pain on other people because the person with authority told them it was ok.

One of the reasons this particular experiment became so famous was because of the (unsubstantiated) rumours of the group of participants asking the questions went on to suffer from extreme PTSD, because they thought they'd inflict such severe pain on other people.

Many of them were rumoured to have committed suicide because of it. History gives us far too many examples of where authority has been used to convince ordinary people to commit horrific acts against other people.

There are less severe examples every day in the workplace.

How many people do you know who have had relationships end because of the amount of time they spend at work?

It may even have happened to you.

Very few people actually want to put their careers ahead of their families, but their bosses – the people with authority – have told them it's the only way to get ahead.

Those people often experience burnout and mental health issues because they don't have the harmony a more balanced attitude brings.

The good news is authority can also be used as a force for good. If the person with authority has the intent to always make people and their lives better, they can create a highly resilient workforce capable of excellence.

They do this by telling and showing people it's ok to open up, it's ok to try new things, it's ok to be themselves, it's also ok to be held to account and hold others to account.

All these things are ok because the intent is to make people and their lives better, and people will respond accordingly.

CONSISTENCY

A leader who acts with **consistency** is a leader who immediately reduces chaos and confusion from the workplace.

A leader who changes their mood, style, approach as often as the weather has a workforce who simply doesn't know when and if they should raise issues or difficulties with them.

This doubt disconnects leaders from their workforce, introduces mistrust, and ultimately lowers performance – it makes them a dick! Being consistent provides a platform for trust and respect to be built, and ultimately increases performance. Note the deliberate phraseology.

Consistency provides a platform for trust and respect to be built from, but doesn't develop it without further work.

LIKING

This is the 2nd most dangerous form of persuasion in this writer's opinion. Leaders with a natural charisma have a deep psychological impact on other people. We want to be liked by them.

It's not enough that we like them; we have a need for them to know who we are and for them to like and respect us. This doesn't necessarily happen at a conscious level, often is unconscious.

We do things for them, agree with them, we'll go along with their ideas and plans, even if we have better ideas, or don't like what it is we're being asked to do. We still do it because at a subconscious level, we don't want to risk disappointing them, and them not liking us.

Think this sounds farfetched? Two of the most charismatic leaders of the 20th century were Adolf Hitler and Heinrich Himmler. People loved them.

Look at what they were able to influence ordinary, everyday people, just like you and I, to do.

They're not the only examples either. History is littered with leaders who have charisma and intelligence and use it to convince ordinary people to commit horrific acts.

This method of influence can be dangerous in a much less severe way too. Leaders who aren't blessed with a natural charisma and try to make people like them, rather than let it happen naturally can very easily lose the respect of the workforce.

A lack of respect is a great foundation for mistrust to grow. I've seen far too many leaders over the years try to gain respect by saying yes to every request, and try to be liked by never holding their teams to account for low standards or poor quality.

This is a recipe for false harmony and doesn't make people or their lives better.

Leaders gain respect for doing what's right, not what's easy. Often the right decision will upset people. But, if they trust that your intention is always to make people and their lives better, they'll accept short-term disappointment because they respect that you're doing your best.

CONSENSUS

The final principle of influence presented by Cialdini was that of **consensus**. Cialdini surmised that if you're able to convince the majority, or at least the key personnel, this consensus will persuade everyone else to follow suit.

Within a team dynamic, leaders often allow themselves to become overwhelmed by not only giving everyone a voice, but also trying to please everyone. This comes from a false belief that in order to please people you have to go along with their idea.

But everyone has different ideas, therefore decision making is stifled, delayed, or just doesn't happen, because there's no way to please everyone.

This results in chaos, confusion, overwhelm, missed targets, loss of bonuses etc., just because the leader was trying to please everyone. What a dick, ey?!

What the studies show us though, is people don't need the idea chosen to be theirs, they just need to be heard and to understand why the final decision was made.

All leaders need to do is allow everyone to have their opinion heard, then explain the final decision.

By doing this they'll be able to influence either the majority or at least key players to get behind them.

This consensus will make it easier for the naysayers to get on board. By being decisive, it allows the team to work productively and efficiently. It gives them the best chance of hitting deadlines, achieving their targets, and gaining their bonuses/incentives.

The leader's no longer a dick!

UNITY

Unity wasn't part of the original Cialdini methods of influence, but it was added in 2016. He stated that we are more influenced by someone we share a sense of identity with.

Cialdini stated that family ties are often the strongest form of unity; next are shared ties such as a favourite sports team or shared hobby.

In the workplace, leaders can create a sense of unity by recruiting based on a strong set of moral values. A team with a shared vision of success, who share the same purpose and values are a team that will perform to exceptional levels because of the unity – the sense of belonging – they feel.

Human beings have a deep psychological need for the group they belong to be the best. So, when they feel as though they belong in a team, they will do everything they can to see it succeed and be the best.

Post-chapter activity: Reflection

Consider all the types of persuasion presented by Cialdini. Not all of them will be relevant to your circumstances.

Of the ones that could work, how could you implement them, to be a positive source of influence for your staff?

Leadership is a paradox; it's simultaneously really simple and incredibly complex.

Chapter 4

Bias, Discrimination, and Responsible Leadership

Now that we're communicating, listening, and influencing effectively, it's time to start looking internally at the thing that will most severely impact your ability to lead effectively - bias.

It'll be very easy at this point to say something along the lines of "I'm not biased". It's an easy self-assessment to make, the truth is more likely that you don't discriminate. Everyone one us is biased in one form or another.

According to the Oxford English dictionary, the definition of Bias is: "an inclination or prejudice, for or against one person or group. Especially in a way considered unfair".

Whilst their definition of discrimination is: "the practice of treating somebody, or a particular group in society, less fairly than others".

At first glance, the two definitions seem pretty similar, when the specific wording is compared though, they are very different.

Bias is an **inclination** either in the positive or negative sense. Bias is passive, there is no action taken when operating in bias alone.

Discrimination is **actively treating** someone, or a group, negatively. Discrimination is more active than bias, and it only exists in the negative, and it requires action.

Bias is part of the human condition. It's natural and it happens whether we want it to or not. It's actually an extremely important of our psyche.

It helps us form close relationships, and is designed to protect us from perceived threats. It exists within the so called "ancient brain" which society has evolved significantly faster than.

Section 1: Unconscious Bias and its Effects

Here are a couple of examples of how both a positive and a negative bias may be formed.

Think of the group of friends you spent the most amount of time with while growing up. Think of the characteristic they all shared. It may be shared hobbies and interests, it could be a similar taste in music, film, or fashion.

It could be that you all belonged to the same sports club, or supported the same football team. It could be that you were all the "nerdy" kids.

It doesn't matter what that shared characteristic was, the important thing is that you all shared it. Because you felt safe within that group, you will have developed a positive bias towards anyone who you recognise that shared characteristic within.

There's a good chance that you feel yourself drawn to them, wanting to like, and be liked by them. If you're their boss, there's a good chance you treat them with more leniency and provide them with better opportunities.

This isn't something you deliberately do, you don't consciously decide to let them off the hook, or think they're better than anyone else. Your subconscious is making you behave this way without you realising it.

Now for the negative example. There are a couple of ways in which a negative bias can occur within us.

First of all, from those people who were the biggest influence on us growing up. Between the ages of 2 and 7, we are at our most susceptible to external influence.

That's because our intelligence is starting to grow, and we absorb information like sponges.

The problem is that our intelligence hasn't yet grown to the point where we question what we're told. If our parents, grandparents, or those people we feel closest to at that age, have particularly strong opinions, those opinions are firmly planted within us.

These are the people that keep us safe, warm, fed, and comforted. We believe every word they say to us because we haven't learned to question them, and from a deep psychological level, we want to believe them because of what we get from them.

If they have strong negative opinions towards people or groups with certain characteristics, those opinions are embedded within us too.

As we get older, and our ability to question others' thoughts and opinions grows, and if we're lucky enough to have experiences that challenge those negative thoughts, we can prevent ourselves from being actively discriminate.

However, because those thoughts and opinions were embedded within us during our most influential, our ancient brain, that doesn't have the ability of rationale thought, will still have a negative bias against those characteristics.

Another way in which a negative bias can be developed is that of active experience.

Consider where you grew up or went to school. Was there a particular group that you actively avoided? They could be a group in the neighbourhood who were reputedly responsible for most of the street crime. Or it could be a group who bullied you at school, or who you had a particular rivalry with.

That group will have a shared characteristic that your ancient brain has identified as a threat.

Whilst consciously, as you get older, you learn that not everyone with those characteristics is a threat, the ancient brain doesn't have the ability to think in that rational way. It just remembers threat or no threat.

As the ancient brain exists within the subconscious, we're very rarely aware that we have biases. This lack of awareness means we can't control them, and they result in us making decisions, or behaving in a way, that can appear to be discriminatory.

Have you ever known someone who's faced a tribunal, or disciplinary process because of discriminatory behaviour?

Did they argue vehemently that they don't discriminate?

There's a very good chance that their behaviour stemmed from an unconscious bias. They're actually probably right that they're not a discriminatory person, but their lack of self-awareness resulted in their subconscious influencing them to make decisions, or behave in a way, that another person or group, found unfair.

Bias also exists in the same part of the brain as feeling and emotion.

Have you ever wondered why it's so difficult to express feelings and emotions, without some vague, superficial, cliché?

It's because our language centre operates in a completely different part of the brain – the logical centre if you will – and those two parts of the brain don't talk.

To add some context to that, think of the person you love the most in the world. Now try to think of what it is about them that you love so much. Write those words or phrases down.

Next, think of those words in isolation, how many other people can you associate those words or phrases with? There's a good chance that there's many other people those words can describe, but you don't have romantic or intimate feelings towards them.

This is because when we are asked to describe why we love someone, we immediately engage with the logical part of the brain, that doesn't have access to the emotions. So, we end up using vague, superficial, language that describes numerous people.

Section 2: Overcoming Bias: Acting without Prejudice

This inability to articulate our feelings properly can actually help us to identify what our subconscious biases may be.

Try to think of someone, or a group of people, that you're unsure of. It's not necessarily that you don't like them, you're just not sure you can trust them, but you don't know why. They've never done anything negative towards you, or they've never made mistakes that are any worse than other people that you don't have negative feelings, or misgivings, towards.

This inability to articulate in a coherent manner is a great indicator that they have a characteristic that you have a negative bias towards.

If there's a group of people you feel this way about, there's a good chance that you either have multiple bias, or they all share the same characteristic that you're negatively disposed to.

The danger with this approach in the in-built self-protection aspect of the human psyche.

As human beings we don't like to admit anything negative about ourselves. Both our conscious and unconscious minds are going to do everything it can to sabotage our increase in self-awareness.

It's going to come up with excuses as to why we don't trust that person or people. Or it's going to point to positive things you may have done for that person or people.

Remember, bias isn't the same as discrimination. You cannot help being biased, it's something our mind does, without our realisation, to try to protect us. The fact that you may have done something positive for someone, doesn't mean you're not biased against them.

How did you feel when you did that thing?

Did you do it begrudgingly, or only because you had to?

These feelings are strong indicators of bias.

Other methods of identifying bias are through professional assessments. There are many psychological assessments that give you indicators of what your biases might be, some are free, others can be quite expensive.

Harvard University has a free online IAT (Implicit Association Test), that could give you indicators of what your biases might be.

Note the deliberately vague language there. An IAT is a research tool, not a diagnostic one. The results should not be used as an absolute diagnosis – Harvard tell you that themselves in the test introduction. As an indicator of potential biases though, it's quite useful.

Ultimately though, as human beings, let alone as leaders, our biases, and associated unconscious behaviour is one of the strongest ways other people will see us as dicks. In the workplace, especially when you have leadership responsibility, being seen as a dick because of lack of self-awareness of our biases, is the absolute best we can hope for.

Worst case scenario is that we end of losing our jobs – and chances of future employment – because of unconscious behaviour related to our biases.

There is good news though. When we accept that we will have biases, and we actively raise our self-awareness of what they might be, we can do something about them.

Firstly, we can slow our decision making down. We can ask ourselves why we're taking this action – whether it be denying someone's request, or giving extra responsibility to someone else.

We can ask ourselves what evidence we have that suggests person A should get the promotion instead of person B. We can ask, are we making this decision based on fact or feeling? We can challenge ourselves to look for positive evidence for person B as well as person A.

We can also challenge ourselves to look for negative evidence for person A as well as person B. When we actively ask ourselves these questions, we can bypass the emotional centres, which is where bias exists, and engage with the logical centres.

This helps us make rational, intelligent, fully considered decisions that stand up to scrutiny and gives us the best chance possible of giving the right responsibility to the right person, not just the person we feel more positively disposed to.

Post-chapter activity:

Do an internet search for an Implicit Association Test (IAT) to assess your internal bias.

Point to note: an IAT is not a diagnosis, it's a research tool. It won't tell you what biases you DO have, just what you MIGHT have.

As a free tool to increase your self-awareness, it's a useful exercise.

If you have a budget, there are paid assessments, conducted by professionals that will give you more definitive results.

Caution: you may find out something about yourself that you do not like. Sharing that information with people who don't fully understand the nature of bias could have detrimental effects on your relationships with them.

You don't get to call yourself a leader, that's for others to decide.

Chapter 5

Attitude & Behaviour: The Interplay of Mindsets

I can remember summer of 2003. I was part of a joint RAF & Royal Artillery unit based in Woolwich Barracks in South London. I was an RAF SAC (Senior Aircraftman), which is a junior rank - 1 level senior to entry level.

One afternoon I needed to visit Regimental Headquarters to see the administrative officer. I'd never been there before, so my only thoughts were "where am I, and where is his office?"

Going down a long corridor with lots of offices on either side, not really looking at who was around me, just looking for the right office. I passed someone I didn't know and was immediately berated for having a bad attitude!

My crime? I didn't address him as Sir as I passed him.

I can't blame him entirely; the culture of the Army was that of acknowledging people of senior rank whenever you passed them. It's a mark of respect for the rank. My experience in the RAF was that it wasn't an expected (or at least enforced) etiquette.

I wasn't deliberately being rude; I was just preoccupied with looking for where I was going. I was mortified by this berating.

It was embarrassing, I was confused, and being accused of having a bad attitude resulted in me actually having one.

Knowing what I know now, his attitude was probably more about what was going on with him, rather than me.

To be completely transparent, I was in the wrong. I was aware of the etiquette, I'd just lost sight of it because it was new to me and I was lost. His actions far exceed my crime.

It's likely that there were many other factors at play, me not acknowledging him was just the straw that broke the camel's back.

The term "attitude" is one that has a lot of bias associated with it. We regularly consider the term bad attitude. Often though, someone's attitude is determined by a number of factors.

For example, if I was to wake up in the morning feeling unwell, or after a poor night's sleep, I may go into a meeting in less than my best state of mind. I may mindlessly speak or act in a way that creates thoughts in other people's heads such as "he's got a bad attitude" or "what a dick!"

What's equally likely, my poor mindset means that I'd be far more likely to see a poor attitude in others.

Think of the last time you thought someone had a bad attitude. What was it they were doing, or did, that provoked that reaction within you?

Another thought to consider is, what was going on with you that could have provoked that reaction in you.

Mindset is hugely complex, with many factors and layers that affect it. Put simply though, if we're in a positive mindset, we tend to see the positive things in the world, or in people. If we're in a negative mindset, we tend to only see the negative.

This is because the human mind looks for what it wants to see.

Have you ever played the game 'spot the coloured car'?

You think of the most obscure colour car then challenge your kids, or passengers, to count how many they can see within a certain time frame. Whoever sees the most, wins.

When playing the game did you notice that no matter how obscure a colour you choose, you always find some.

This is because you've told your brain that you want to see that colour, so it prioritises that colour being seen.

There's an awful lot of biological facts behind this tendency, but as I'm not a biologist, I won't give it the credit it deserves by attempting to explain it.

Section 1: The Complex Nature of Attitude

Our mindset and attitude work in the same way as that game. As human beings we will always have ups and downs. When we're up, our mindset tends to be positive. When we're down, our mindset is far more negative.

Another factor of human beings is that we like to be right. We want our mindset to be the right one, so we look for evidence to prove that we're right to feel the way we do.

It's not that the evidence that suggests the opposite is true isn't there, but as we're specifically looking for evidence to prove we're right, our minds prioritise allowing us to see that.

When we're in a positive mindset, it's very easy to see positivity around us. We see the good in people, we see what they're doing well, and we're quick to point out all of the positives.

This helps us be seen as a good person, with a good attitude, and a likeable person. If we hold leadership responsibility in the workplace, it's much easier for us to be seen as a good leader.

Unfortunately, the opposite is also true. When we're experiencing life's downs, our mindset is likely to be negative.

This means we actively seek evidence to prove that we're right. We see negative attitudes in people, we see negative aspects of their work.

Guess what?

This means that we're seen as a negative person, as a poor leader, and ultimately, a dick!

What all this means is that the attitude we see in other people is generally one of two things.

It's an indicator that they're either currently experiencing some sort of struggle in life. Or it's a reflection of the attitude they're seeing in you.

Betari's Box is a fantastic model to explain this.

Section 2: Betari's Box: The Relationship Between Behaviour & Attitude

The model shown in the picture is known as Betari's Box. Its origin is unknown. It's easy to assume that someone named Betari came up with it, but no reference to that individual can be found.

Betari is an ancient Persian city located in the middle of Ancient Mesopotamia. It's also mentioned in both the Quran and the Bible. It's unknown though which, if any, of these link to this model.

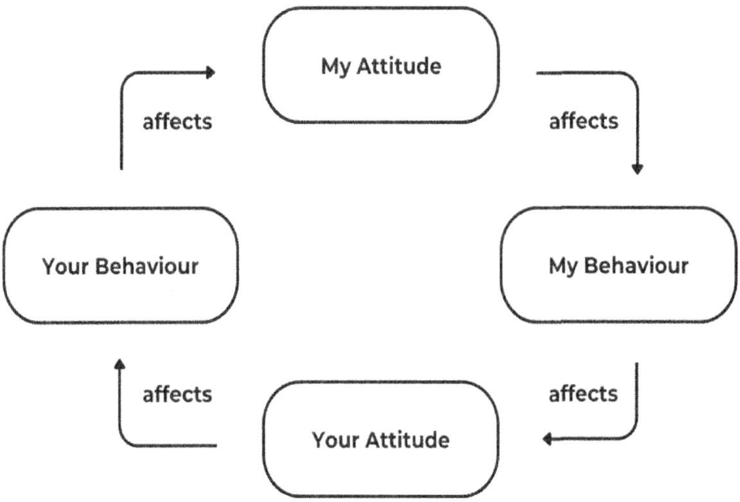

What Betari's Box tells us is that our behaviour reflects the attitude we perceive within someone else. It's linked strongly to bias, because our interpretation of the world exists within the same part of the brain.

As leaders, we need to be mindful of our own state of mind, when communicating with others. If someone unconsciously detects something negative within us, it can affect their behaviour towards us.

Equally, we need to understand that those we're responsible for may be unaware of the effect of their mood on their attitude.

Therefore, we may detect a poor attitude within someone, when actually there's something else affecting the way they're behaving.

Post-chapter activity:

Next time you perceive a negative attitude in someone, check in with yourself. Reflect on what's going on with you; be it at home, at work, or something else. Is there something going on that's affecting your interpretation of that person?

Chapter 6

Leadership vs Management: Identifying the Difference

Moving along our journey of becoming an effective leader, we need to start considering the difference between leadership and management, and identifying what type of leader we are.

There are many types of leader, and styles of leadership. Social Media often presents a biased view that transformational leadership is the "best" style of leadership.

While the science does back up this statement from a one-dimensional perspective, it's not the only style that's effective, and there are many circumstances where it will cause more problems than it solves.

A lot of training providers wrap Leadership & Management together; whilst often the same person has responsibility for both functions, they couldn't be any more different.

To put it simply, a manager concerns themselves with key performance metrics, following policy, performance management processes and ensuring output requirements are met.

It is very easy to be a manager, with absolutely no leadership skills – the reality is, this is often the case. But they're the ones who are often seen as dicks in the workplace.

Often though this is unfair. When leadership and management training is wrapped together, it becomes a one size fits all approach.

When you're dealing with people, this doesn't exist. Leadership training is but one step on the leadership development pathway, and it's not even the first.

Anyone can learn to be a great leader, but it requires an environment where people have the time invested in them and are supported in understanding the different personality types they're responsible for, and how to motivate them.

It takes time, an open mind, and an acceptance at all levels, that occasionally we'll get it wrong.

A leader needs to be mindful of all the management practices, but they rely more on inspiration rather than process.

A leader will find a way to tap into the aspirations of their workforce and help them achieve their ambitions.

Leadership is about finding out what motivates people, how to communicate with them effectively, and how to inspire them to want to perform to the highest possible standards.

Section 1: Balancing People & Tasks

A manager's focus is on the task, a leader's focus is on the people. There is a balance that needs to be achieved though.

People who attempt to be good leaders by focusing entirely on the people, and lose track of the task actually end up failing as a leader and as a manager.

While people who focus entirely on the task are seen as uncaring, concerned only with themselves, and unwilling or unable to think differently.

In John Adair's functional approach to leadership, he identifies three main considerations of any leader.

They are:

1. The team
2. The task
3. The individual

A leader needs to apply equal consideration to each aspect. To do this successfully, sometimes we have to make decisions that seem at odds with one of the other functions.

For example, to ensure the task continues to be achieved in the long term, you may have to reduce team numbers in the short term by sending an individual off on training courses.

Or, you may have an individual who, despite all the right interventions and attempts to assimilate them into the team, they just don't fit.

A hard decision may need to be made that's to the detriment of the individual, but benefits the team and the task.

A common mistake is when a leader attempts to keep all 3 in perfect balance, all of the time. This is impossible.

The reality of leadership is that sometimes a higher priority may need to be placed on one area, such as the task, that could temporarily be to the detriment of the other 2.

The important thing there is to find any opportunity you can to minimise the impact and address the imbalance as soon as you can.

The same can be applied to any of the 3. The important factor is that over time, everything balances itself out.

Section 2: The Tannenbaum-Schmidt Continuum of Leadership

There are lots of different leadership models that explain the different leadership styles a leader can adopt. One of my personal favourites is the Tannenbaum-Schmidt continuum of leadership.

It was developed in 1958 by theorists Robert Tannenbaum and Warren Schmidt. It shows how a manager's approach can range from extreme rigidity at one extreme, to complete abdication at the other.

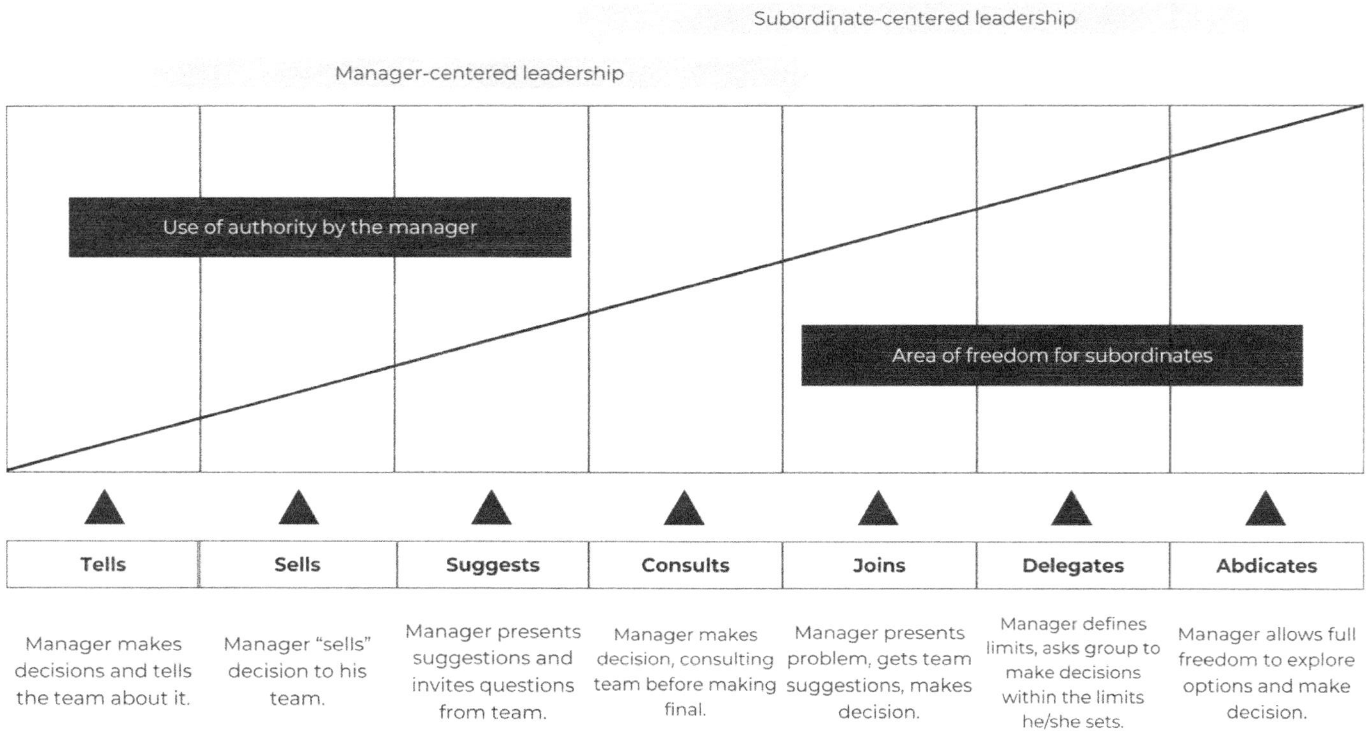
Subordinate-centered leadership
Manager-centered leadership
Use of authority by the manager
Area of freedom for subordinates
Tells
Sells
Suggests
Consults
Joins
Delegates
Abdicates
Manager makes decisions and tells the team about it.
Manager "sells" decision to his team.
Manager presents suggestions and invites questions from team.
Manager makes decision, consulting team before making final.
Manager presents problem, gets team suggestions, makes decision.
Manager defines limits, asks group to make decisions within the limits he/she sets.
Manager allows full freedom to explore options and make decision.

There are other models that use transactional leadership to define the manager centred approach, and transformational as the subordinate centred approach.

Social Media is very good at telling us that we should adopt a transformational style of leadership as often as possible, as it's the "best" way to get full buy-in and the best out of our staff. In reality though, it's just not that simple.

A stereotypical workforce has people of varying degrees of experience and competence.

It has people from multiple different generations, all of whom prefer different styles of leadership, and multiple different personalities who all have very different communication preferences and motivational factors.

Then we have to consider the urgency of the situation and the task at hand.

Whilst those on social media pushing the benefits of transformational leadership are right – it is the best way to help people achieve their full potential. It also takes a lot of time and requires certain competency levels and experience to be fully effective.

Sometimes a more authoritative style of leadership is the best one to adopt. It could be the person responds better to that style, or it could be the urgency of the situation dictates the need.

Ultimately a leader needs to accept there is no one right way to be, they need to be comfortable adapting to a range of styles depending on the person and the situation at the time.

Section 3: Situational Leadership and Adaptive Styles

It's very difficult to apply a fully academic definition to the term situational leadership. Because of the nature of it being situational, all of the factors are constantly changing.

This means a study of it as a leadership style cannot follow a scientific process.

The benefit of this though is we can apply the KISS principle to define it. Situational leadership is simply adapting your style to the demands of the situation. This is what great leaders are able to do. They recognise what the person needs, and balances that against the needs of the situation.

They accept that sometimes the demands of the task dictate the style needed, and can also recognise when there's an opportunity for a more transformational approach and they can develop the skills, competence, and experience of the person.

This is why being seen as a great leader is very hard. It takes great judgement to know the best style for the circumstances; no one can teach great judgement. It comes with experience.

This is why I can guarantee you that you will get it wrong, as your experience builds, there will be times when, despite the greatest of intent, you'll make the wrong judgement call.

You need to give yourself permission for this to happen, and forgiveness when it does.

As long as your intent is the best for the other person or people, that will be recognised. Of course, having some humility and acknowledging your error in judgement will help too.

One of the reasons I prefer the Tannenbaum-Schmidt leadership continuum is that it shows the stages of adaptation, depending on the skills, competence, and experience of the team.

A team full of new, inexperienced people, may need a more authoritative style at the beginning.

But, as their experience and skills grow, a leader can move right, stage by stage, along the continuum, to add more and more autonomy to the team.

Until ultimately, they reach the point at which they have all the skills, competence, and experience necessary to be self-leading.

This then allows the team leader to focus more strategically to create more opportunities for their own development and that of their team members.

Post-chapter activity: Self-reflection

1. What is your natural style of leadership?

2. Under what circumstances could you incorporate any of the other styles?

3. What benefits will this bring?

Chapter 7

Empowerment: Trusting & Developing Others

It's another mark on the buzzword bingo card - Empowerment!

I can't write a book on leadership and not talk about it can I?!

Beyond any leadership tactic, being someone who's able to empower their staff, is going to give you the best chance of creating a team who's high performing, resilient, and who wants to put in 100% for you.

The problem I see regularly is leaders confusing delegation and empowerment. While empowering someone requires delegation, not all delegation is empowering.

When you're delegating work to someone, in essence you're giving them a task that they already know how to do. Something that's already in line with their job description or requirements.

When you empower someone, you're providing the opportunity for growth. You're giving them the authority to learn a new skill, or give them exposure to a higher level of responsibility.

An example of when to empower someone is as a precursor to promotion; a way to develop the skills necessary for promotion so they can hit the ground running when it comes.

As it's a tool for development, and the person being empowered is being given a new responsibility, there is an implied task on the leadership to ensure mentoring and support is available.

The definition of empowerment, according to the Oxford English dictionary, is "authority or power given to someone to do something".

Empowerment, when used correctly, is a great tool any leader can use to create exceptional teams. It provides you capacity to focus on higher level tasks, whilst also developing the skill sets of the individuals you're responsible for.

The definition of empowerment though is far too simplistic for the workplace. For it to be effective, it is not simply a case of giving the authority to complete a task, it requires far more than that.

For empowerment to be effective, we need to give our individuals some STD – in reverse:

1. **Delegation**. This is the first stage of empowerment – actually providing the authority for completing a task.

2. **Trust**. The second stage, once a task or responsibility has been delegated, is to trust them. This means letting go of control, accepting that it probably won't be done the same way as you do it, but that doesn't mean it's wrong.

   Providing someone with the authority to complete a task, or take on additional responsibility means allowing them to be themselves and work in the way that's right to them.

3. **Supervision**. While we as leaders delegate authority to complete a task or hold responsibility, we don't abdicate responsibility for the output. That remains with us.

   The level of supervision we provide will depend on the amount of trust we have in the individual, or their level of experience, but oversight is still necessary. The trick is being able to maintain the balance between being an empowering leader, and a micromanager.

Section 1: Balancing Trust & Supervision

As with integrity, we don't get to decide whether or not we're a micro-manager, that's down to the interpretation of the people we're responsible for.

Each individual will not only need different levels of supervision, but they'll also have their own idea of what is micro-management and what isn't.

A useful tactic to employ when empowering people is to have a set of agreements.

Agreeing in advance what the boundaries they can operate within i.e., what decisions they're able to make without senior approval, how much they're able to spend per transaction and in total, or any other criteria that's appropriate to your workplace.

Once that's been established, having an agreed 'check-in' frequency will allow you to keep track of progress, realign and/or rectify any diversions or mistakes, and provide guidance where necessary.

When these check-ins are pre-agreed, the individuals won't feel as though they're being micro-managed, because you're doing what they agreed to.

The more skill, experience, and trust an individual has, the looser the boundaries, and the less frequent the check-ins can be.

The check-ins also allow you to identify if you've been too strict, or too relaxed, and adapt as necessary.

Post-chapter activity:

Who amongst your staff is giving indicators that they need a new challenge?

What can you empower them with to re-engage them, improve their motivation, and improve their prospects under your leadership?

Chapter 8

Emotional Intelligence: Harnessing Emotions for Success

As we move into the last couple of chapters, it's time to consider some of the more unconscious factors that contribute to effective leadership.

By unconscious, I mean the emotional factors that we have no direct control over, and hugely impact the way other people interpret and respond to us.

Emotional intelligence (otherwise known as Emotional Quotient or EQ) is the ability to understand, use, and manage your own emotions in positive ways to relieve stress, communicate effectively, empathise with others, overcome challenges, and defuse conflict.

What I find interesting about that definition is the focus on your own emotions.

Now, don't get me wrong. As a leader, being aware of your own emotions, how they affect our attitude, our behaviour, and influence the attitude and behaviour in others is vital.

However, understanding the emotions of other people is equally important.

Has anyone ever used words with you to the effect of: "leave your home life at home, and your work life at work"? That's actually nonsense. There is not one aspect of life that doesn't affect others.

If your home life is perfect, but your work life is miserable, it won't take long for the emotions associated with the workplace start affecting the way you respond to your partner, kids, etc.

Likewise, if your workplace is a great place to be, but you're struggling at home, it won't be long before the emotions from home start becoming a distraction at work, which affects your work quality.

A leader with a good EQ level understands this, and provides opportunities for their team members to regulate their emotions which ensures there is minimal effect on the workplace.

Conversely, when we as individuals, let alone as leaders, understand emotions properly, we can come up with agreements at home that allow for an output of emotion, in a non-judgemental way.

This will help to minimise the impact a bad day at work has at home.

This recognition of our emotions, and the impact they can have on others, can help us to understand the emotions of other people.

When we hold leadership responsibility, and we understand the effect of emotion, we can provide the support necessary which gives us the best chance of success.

Section 1: The Power of Emotional Intelligence

Increasing your EQ, as with anything that contributes to great leadership, is not easy. The fact that it relies on us controlling our emotions, when it's often our emotions that control us, indicates the practice and self-discipline needed.

There are 4 key areas that a good level of emotional intelligence will benefit.

Self-management. You're able to control impulsive feelings and behaviours, manage your emotions in healthy ways, take initiative, follow through on commitments, and adapt to changing circumstances.

Self-awareness. You recognize your own emotions and how they affect your thoughts and behaviour. You know your strengths and weaknesses and have self-confidence.

Social awareness. You have empathy. You can understand the emotions, needs, and concerns of other people, pick up on emotional cues, feel comfortable socially, and recognize the power dynamics in a group or organisation.

Relationship management. You know how to develop and maintain good relationships, communicate clearly, inspire and influence others, work well in a team, and manage conflict.

Control and expertise of these four areas will really accelerate your leadership ability to new heights.

Post-chapter activity:

What opportunities are available in your workplace that provide the opportunity for your staff to regulate their emotions?

What else could work?

“Leadership is not a license to do less, it's a responsibility to do more.”
– Simon Sinek

Chapter 9

Ethos & Integrity: Aligning Values & Actions

The final chapter of the book is arguably one of the most important. It doesn't matter how good your personal leadership skills are; if the culture at your organisation is a negative one, it's going to be very difficult for your staff to feel engaged and fulfilled.

Most companies have a set of values; values are created to drive the organisational culture that's desired. The mistake I've seen over, and over, again, is the values have been created, but they're not enforced.

How often have you worked for a company, or an organisation, who have a defined set of corporate values, but they're just ignored? They may be plastered all over the walls, on recruitment material, on the website, everywhere!

But the lived experience is that nobody – including the leadership – actually applies them.

There are few better ways of being seen as a bit of a dick, than ticking the values box, but not actually living by them.

Values can't just be words that sound good. A true value is something you believe deep down in your core.

A proper value is something that makes you feel dirty if you don't live by it; it's something you strive to live by every single day.

A common mistake people make when setting their values is they choose a singular word. Common examples are integrity, determination, honesty, etc. What does the term integrity mean to you?

According to CS Lewis, it means doing the right thing, even when no one's looking. The Oxford English Dictionary defines it as: 'the quality of being honest and having strong moral principles'.

To me, it means doing what's right, not what's easy. I'm not a betting man, but I'd be willing to bet my mortgage that many of you will have slightly different interpretations of what it means to you.

This is the problem with singular word values, the nuances of the different interpretations of their meaning, resulting in people not applying the intent of the value when it was set.

Having values that are statements rather than single words, makes it much easier for people to understand, and therefore, live by.

For example, my company values are:

1. We do what's right, not what's easy.

2. There is no one size fits all approach to leadership.

3. Everyone knows something we don't.

4. Learning needs to be enjoyed to be effective.

The single words these statements were developed from are:

1. Integrity

2. Flexibility

3. Humility

4. Fun

By expanding them into statements, the ambiguity is removed. I can hold myself to account for living and working by them, and as I scale my business, I can use them as a basis to recruit from, as a motivational driver, and as a way to hold team members to account if standards slip.

You don't need to be a business owner to establish a set of values you hold yourself and your team members accountable to.

It doesn't matter if you're a CEO, or newly promoted supervisor, or any level in-between.

By identifying what your values are, you can make it clear what your behavioural expectations are, what the standards you expect are, and when you recruit based on your values, you can use them to get all team members aligned to a single vision.

The bigger the organisation, the harder it is for the top-level corporate values to be meaningful to everyone employed there.

Department heads, managers, team leaders, and supervisors, should all be free to set their own values in order to bring the team(s) together.

As long as they're aligned to corporate values, you'll still be able to meet the corporate expectations, while working to a set of values that are meaningful to you and your team(s).

Section 1: The Subjectivity of Ethos

Ethos is an ancient Greek word that means character. It's our character that defines what our ethics are, within leadership though, ethics are entirely subjective.

They're personal, and the way we interpret them can differ from person to person. Sometimes that difference is only very subtle, sometimes it's huge.

Integrity is a term that is linked strongly to ethos. The Oxford English dictionary definition of integrity is "the quality of being honest and having strong moral principles". But whose moral principles are used to determine if someone has integrity? Yours? Other people's?

The worst despots and dictators in human history will say that they had integrity.

They acted in accordance with their own ethics, so it could be argued that they did have integrity. But people whose moral values differ, will argue they didn't.

Section 2: Consistency & Accountability

It's for reasons such as this that a leader's moral values, ethos, and actions need to remain consistent at all times.

We can't claim to have integrity if we state that we value punctuality, but are regularly late to meetings and appointments.

When our values, ethics, and behaviour are aligned though, we have a powerful leadership tool at our disposal.

When we're able to align our team(s) to a single vision, and a shared set of values, we can keep each other accountable without conflict or blame. We can create efficiencies that contribute to high output and strong rapport.

Post-chapter activity: Organisational survey

A company culture isn't what you say it is. It's the way people feel on a Sunday evening before they go back to work on the Monday.

How can you survey all your staff to learn the truth about your company culture? What could you do with that information?

“Leadership is not about being in charge, it's about taking care of those in your charge.”

– Simon Sinek

Conclusion

The Power of Respectful Leadership

Thank you for reading this book "Leadership 101: Don't be a Dick".

My hope in writing this book is for readers to have a reference guide on how to lead effectively.

I've simplified many of the subjects I've written about purely for ease of interpretation, and for leaders to be able to contextualise them into their reality.

I believe that the best leadership training in the world won't produce great leaders.

Great trainers will create a positive learning environment, which is inclusive and encourages everyone to contribute and learn effectively.

The trouble is, training alone is objective. Training that's accredited to qualifications requires that everyone receiving that training follows the same training objectives, key knowledge requirements etc. This means it's a one-size-fits-all solution and the reality of the individuals is lost.

I used to provide leadership & management training for the RAF. In my (admittedly biased) opinion, the training we provided there was second to none. It was world class.

Despite the world class training we provided, I was concerned by the sheer number of stories detailing such horrific leadership, by people who had received this great training.

The more I learned as to why this might be, the more I realised that leadership is subjective. It is nuanced depending on the personality of the person leading, the personalities of the people they're leading, the individual circumstances of everyone involved, and the situation the business is in.

What's needed is ongoing support tailoring the development to the individual's bespoke needs.

I hope the simplification of the theories I've written about, will help leaders to contextualise them to their reality, helping them to avoid the label of "toxic leader".

The theories I've written about aren't mine, they were all designed by people far cleverer than I am. Many of them may not be new to you either.

If you've been lucky enough to have had investment made in your leadership development, you'll probably have learned about them before.

Of course, there are many other theories out there too. Their exclusion from this book isn't to suggest they're not worth learning.

These are the ones I'm familiar with, use in the training I deliver, and reference in my 1:1 work when helping leaders understand how they can use their personalities, traits, and strengths to become the leaders they're capable of being.

We have explored many of the theories that will help you to nurture positive workplace relationships.

By visiting the common principles, covered by many Leadership & Management training courses - an oxymoron in itself, as they're two very different things - you'll have all the information, that once applied, to be considered a respectful and effective leader.

Of course, Neuroscience tells us that when reading a book, or attending a training course, we engage the logical part of the brain.

Leadership is about people, talking to them, dealing with them, managing, & developing them. Because of the way the brain and our psyche are structured, when interacting with the world, we operate from the emotional centre for the first 5-15 seconds.

The emotional and logical sides of the brain don't communicate; all the learning you do through books, courses, etc, doesn't feature in our initial interactions.

That means that if those first 5-15 seconds are perceived by the emotional centre as a threat, the rest of the interaction won't go well either.

This is normal human psychology, and only those with extreme skills at emotional management can ride that out.

There is good news though; we can create emotional memories. We do it all the time. Those people we have consistently positive interactions with, are people our emotional centre - Chimp Brain in Prof Steve Peters' model - has already deemed them as non-threatening.

All we need to do is have the courage to start practising the ideas this book presents.

When we do, and they go well, we'll create neural pathways that help us to navigate those initial interactions with a positive attitude.

This makes it far easier to create workplaces that are empathetic and empowering. A place where individuals thrive, and teams excel.

When you're able to keep the idea of not being a dick front and centre of your mind, and learn to apply yourself according to your values, we can transform the workplace into a positive and inclusive environment and make a lasting impact as a leader.

Thanks for reading. If you'd like information on the support available to improve yours, or your organisation's leadership, please visit www.onedegree.uk.

Printed in Great Britain
by Amazon

48382045R00066